Entrepreneur From Zero

I0504202

George Freeman

WHY ENTREPRENEUR FROM ZERO

Stop postponing your dreams, and your dream life. Entrepreneurial life is around the corner, thanks to the internet and the way the internet has connected people and businesses.

Now it is easier than ever to find which business is hot and emerging at the click of a button, which business venture is going to be successful without putting time and energy.

This gem of a guide book for your entrepreneurial journey will tell you how you can get started with your startup from nothing.

Yes it is possible to start building your startup and generate income streams with literally zero dollars investment.

This isn't a book which will ask you to put upfront ten thousand dollars and a year and create the billion dollar app only to find out that it has no takers!

CONTENTS

10   Let's Get Started

PREFACE

Stop Postponing and get started building your startup and income streams from no investment at all.

In this guide book you will learn how to create simplest businesses from nothing, find out what is going to sell before you invest any time and energy in a venture.

How to create passive streams of income and grow from nothing.

Building a 1000 dollar income stream each month that gives great cash flow is within everyone's reach! Heck this entire business was made out of nothing and is generating five figures each month, learn from a serial entrepreneur with over a 100 ventures under his belt.

The biggest thing this book teaches you is that you don't need to have a lot of capital to get started with your dream life of being an Entrepreneur.

It will tell you the key things to survive in today's cut throat business environment.

1 START SELF PUBLISHING FROM ZERO

Okay so this is not like the regular text books which will give you page after page of motivation, that you can always find at my blog https://freemanfromzero.wixsite.com/mysite

And why would you pay for free knowledge, in this book I will give you concrete examples on how to get started with generating income from day 1 and with zero investment and how to be an entrepreneur.

So when I started I was in a regular job, with the usual debt and working in a cubicle and I decided enough was enough. I can't work for others no more, and anyways whatever I get is a fraction of my efforts.

It is time to get full value for my time and efforts.

I logged on to the internet and figured I would self publish using the Amazon Kindle platform.

I enrolled on http://kdp.amazon.com and I signed up for other free web publishers like Smashwords, Draft2Digital and PublishDrive. Later I would figure out how difficult the publishing process on Smashwords would be and would only use Amazon, Google Publisher as my preferred publishers.

Also, I later found out that Amazon Kindle Publisher program coupled with having my own website would be the most profitable thing.

But this book is starting from zero and I would not tell that you spend 30 to 50 dollars getting your domain, hosting and setting up wordpress.

It is time to really start from scratch. You are good at something, all these years you must be knowing something that others know less of, you may have some skills, or you may have something that you would be passionate about.

And of this thing that either you are passionate about or you are really good and knowledgeable you start creating notes.

You create a blueprint as to how a person go from point A to point B, you need to create a bridge that will take the person from point A of having a dream that he wants to be good to point B of having achieved that dream.

You need to give this cue to the people, that you have the thing or the bridge that will take them to point B and once you put that on a marketplace like Amazon, people will study it and if they think it worthy they will buy.

Let me show one example from my sales page.

Royalties Earned (What's this?) ▾

Currency	eBook Royalty	Paperback Royalty	KU/KOLL Royalty	Total Royalty
USD	3,495.74	12,554.50	289.37	16,339.61
GBP	143.64	1,127.22	37.89	1,308.75
EUR	773.70	915.13	37.28	1,726.11
JPY	4,009.00	0.00	31.78	4,040.78
INR	2,544.22	0.00	79.56	2,623.78
CAD	225.24	0.00	2.76	228.00
BRL	193.85	0.00	15.37	209.22
MXN	1,750.00	0.00	2.15	1,752.15
AUD	125.41	0.00	0.17	125.58

It may not be fully visible above but it will give you an idea, I was able to make sales in Amazon from self published material which I put down in Microsoft Word, got an ebook template from Google and published it using Amazon KDP's automated software tool.

Remember I was not a writer, but in the first month I made 50 dollars, in the second month I made 200 dollars, and I was able to get enough for my website.

The Kindle program enables anyone to make money from eBook contents starting 25 pages.

And let me tell you it is really easy for anyone to create a simple course book and a simple guidebook which will act as a bridge for others.

Take this book for an example the crux that I am selling you is that you can start with no investment and get started on entrepreneurship. It gives you real methods which I or others have used to create passive incomes.

Of course why would you pay for motivational stuff which the interent is so full of it, so I am giving you all the proof and real world examples, with real income proof that I have done it and you can follow in these footsteps to get a thousand dollars and from that how to scale it up.

Ok so the first point is that you create your own Publishing account with various publishers.

Now create a blog using this blog you can validate if people are interested in your topic or not.

If people are interested and they are willing to sign up and pay for a freebie, it is highly likely they are going to pay for your course.

Now it does not have to be in your name

as well, you can select a pen name and with that you can even hide your identity.

You will also need to create social media accounts using that you are going to spread the word about your course.

There is even a KDP promotional scheme where you can buy ads if you want to scale up.

So you have created your first course and you are marketing it, and everyone that you know you are buying them free copies and having them give a review.

This is essential, unless people know that something is good, they are not going to spend their hard earned bucks on it.

You need to get your course reviewed positively by at least twenty people who will find good things in that, and will tell the world, of course I would not recommend this to you in the early phase as we are starting from zero.

So you can start giving your course for free and in the first two months you will get enough people who will have viewed your course and some would have reviewed it, it is imperative that you need to bring out a fully polished course, otherwise if you start getting negative reviews it is not going to sell.

So let's say in the first 2 months you generate 250 dollars and it is not hard to do. If your content is worth it, and people need it, they are going to pay for it, of course you will need to havily market it and do everything you can do to let the world know that this exists, now either you create a Youtube video, or a youtube channel, or a blog, or a social media account or you have friends that will help is your strategy. And it is upto you how you promote it.

But once it is up and small amount of revenue is coming to your bank, it is time to scale up, get a domain name, get hosting, and buy this book to some friends for free and get them review it.

This is the starting of the momentum.

You have made a small ball of ice and you roll it down the mountain in such a way that it keeps getting bigger and bigger and keeps attracting more ice, that's the key idea.

You alone cannot generate that momentum, that momentum will be generated when enough people know about it, they discuss it, they comment on it, if it is a great effort they will tell others about it which will make it a momentum or probably a viral thing.

This is a good thing because if this happens your product will sell, your self published course will sell like hot cakes.

Let me give an example there was a guy in a regular normal accounting job and he thought of creating a manual on how the layman can understand accounting concepts and his course started selling like hotcakes, he became on the top 10 book list for accounting manual and he in his own words says that the amount of money he made from that book is like what he would have made from an entrepreneurial venture.

In actuality he made upwards of 200,000 dollars in the very first year and now you tell me isn't that great!

If my book is being read by say ten million people then I would like thousands to achieve similar and these are the odds if you are going to follow my advice and you are going to create gems of products, people are going to buy.

People are looking for great courses, there are so many people in the world today with their bank accounts attached to amazon accounts that if they see a good thing they will buy.

IF you can do some research say you are doing a research and condensifying material for people, like it may take a month for people to find this information and you are researching, making notes and giving them everything condensed as a single course, it is going to save people so much time.

And they are going to pay for it, they are going to progress because of your efforts and this is real value, real value you are going to get paid.

So if you want to start from nothing a very good way is to create a blog and an eBook in the form of a course, this you publish it for say 3 or 4 dollars and it is not a hindrance to the majority of people to pay that price. If the content is there people will pay for it.

So very soon say in six months you might have several courses down the line and you can generate a passive stream of 500 or 1000 dollars upwards depending on how great your course is and how great your marketing strategy is.

If anytime you are stuck in doing this you know that help is around the corner and you can contact me at FreemanFromZero@gmail.com of course my sole goal is to help you achieve success, I am here to take with you private one on one live stream to help you get started up to speed living your dreams for a very reasonable fee.

Now let me tell you you can buy an hour of livestream with me starting just 50 bucks. Email me on how to get started minimum hours that you need to purchase is 3 and let's get started. Just email me with subject line, private one on one so I can send you my packages and payment information. Trust me it is going to really help you earn so much more.

2 DETOUR PRANIC ENERGY

The first step is to bring about a change in your mind, a change in your body, a change in your body, a change in your emotions, a change in your breathing, because that is the blueprint of your life and everything stems from you.
Everything stems from your beliefs, your thoughts, your actions.

The food you eat can either take prana from you, give you prana or be neutral. Which means that the food that you consume is either giving you life, taking away life from you or not acting.

You always want the food to add to your life and well being, however the food that is taking away life from you is being marketed heavily to make you believe it is going to make you happy, or it is going to be healthy.

In a simple sense anything that is natural like vegetables, fruits, cooked dals, wheat, rice, barley, milk that is produced from nature contains pranic energy!

Anything that is man-made, artificial, laced with a lot of sugar, or salt and is kind of junk food or snack is going to take away prana from you for example a pizza, because prana will be needed to process that food from the time you eat to the time you throw it out of your system. It feels easy to eat junk food but it takes a hell lot of energy a hell lot of body processes to throw it out. And if it is not adding to your health it is damaging it.

Neutral food will come in the category where it has little prana and lot of artificial things and the plus and minus are being balanced that the amount of prana that the body will take to throw it out, is the same that you will get out of it. So nothing is being added to your body.

However to live healthily your body needs pranic energy it is needed to maintain liveliness, it is needed to maintain essential bodily functions so everything in the body can work at its peak, if not enough prana is there then the body processes will become weak, the senses may become weak, you may find that you have put on glasses, or that you get tired easily, or decades down the line your body has developed diseases or it has become fat or overweight.

This is so important for you that I had to include this early on. You need a lot of energy in building your startup, money is also energy, people will invest a lot of money in their startups and when you want to start from zero you need to compensate in the form of energy. This needs to be your own energy which will give birth to your business and entrepreneurial venture.

3 STOP WASTING TIME

The first important thing is time. Without time nothing can be achieved. Time is limited in everyone's life. Today everyone has a smartphone. The smartphone can do everything get you food, give you the best 4k gaming experience with players around the world, show you the best movies in 4k and dolby surround sound with no ads, listen to the best music or watch Youtube or see tv shows, live sports from around the world.

It is easy to spend all the time you have on a smartphone, how your 1 day goes, how 10 years will go or how your life will go, you will never know. Smartphone is the best way to guzzle down your free time.

So it is the number 1 killer of time, if you are escapist or want to escape from real world then there are virtual worlds like PUBG or SecondLife where just by using your smartphone you can escape from reality and escape into a new virtual world. But by escaping you are putting a towel on the current problems.

The trouble is you are trapped, you do not know what to do, you do not have a way out, or it is too tough and you do not know how to traverse the rough seas, you are looking for an escape and the smartphone becomes the best device to help you achieve it.

My friends if you keep getting lost, if you keep wasting time, how are you going to be the perfect entrepreneur who is going to add value to the lives of the people. You need to become a producer of value and not a consumer.

You need to give society what is best known to you, you need to give them refined workable solutions, you need to be everything as an entrepreneur, you need to be the visionary, you need to be the architect, you need to be the manager of that solution that people will start using and pay you value.

Let me give an example you take a bridge you pay the toll, it's the same way as an entrepreneur you are building a bridge which is helping solve a problem and you are collecting the toll.

The toll needs to be proportionate to the value being given to the people. If it is a monopoly you can collect as much as you want if it is mandatory for people to cross. So think about it, all government corruption is mainly because of monopoly, this minister or this politician has the power to do what nobody else can do or check, or he can bypass something that law doesn't allow and which will give the other party big gains.

So there are various ways to entrepreneur you need to think about what kind of value you need to provide, if you are able to architect this solution to the people, are people going to use, you need to validate everything, like if you can provide this solution, how much time it will take, do you have the resources to complete that project, is it going to be profitable after your investments.

There is a lot, a lot to think, a lot to do, actually, as an entrepreneur you don't have any time. You won't have any time if you get busy and get started with working.

Rule Number 1

Set a schedule, you need to set work timings, for example as an entrepreneur, you need to set your work timings that you will be working from the time you wake up and get ready to evening, and then you will go work out or go exercise or do the things you like. Once a schedule is fixed then it is easy to allocate time to things that need attention in your career as an entrepreneur.

In this time you need to cut out all time wasters like smartphone watching, useless phone calls, gaming, watching movies, idling time with friends or family etc.

Rule Number 2

The goals needs to be defined and planned, you need to decide what you want to achieve, then you need to decide the most important goals that will help you achieve that and you need to put down the milestones, so that you know where you are, and where you need to go, as it is easy to get lost, and keep avoiding the work which is either difficult, or which is time consuming, people keep putting things off and keep passing time and their time gets absorbed in other wasteful things.

4 How This Super Drug PROVIGIL Made ME a Genius And Helped Earn A Million Dollars

What you have today is what you deserve. It's what YOU are made out. It's always the same equation you = what you have.

Now you equals everything about you, your mind, your decisions, your energy levels, your emotions, your financial IQ.

You don't like it you need to change. Just like for an obese person it is very difficult to lose weight, so is for a person to change himself, most of the times what happens is that a person reverts back to the same individual he was.

Now to bring about a change in you is very easy if you have a very strong will power but most people aren't like that. They are lazy, whimsical, and many times they will do self damaging things well knowing that it may cause them harm.

But if you keep making bad decisions you are going to suffer, now what if I tell you, if you take a performance enhancing drug it is going to change you right from your brain in a most positive way.

You are going to become more intelligent, and if you keep taking this say for a three month period you are going to experience a big change.

Now the equation is changed, you are no longer you, you have become a super You, now what you had doesn't belong to you anymore, that belonged to the normal you, for the super You there is going to be a new life, a new set of things, a new set of value system.

Simply your universe is going to change. When I came to know about this I was sitting on my last pile of 10k dollars, I was suffering big losses, it was the year 2008 and I had with a master day trader who could do no decisions wrong.

I was astounded by him, by his super cars and I was working for him plus day trading on my own.

He knew I was on my last piece of shit and if this thing went down I would be broke, he called me to his cabin and said son, the way you are taking risks, it would make anyone pauper and you never listen to me, you are just chasing losses, chasing is synonymous to breaking the bank.

Listen I will give you Provigil you keep taking it for a week in the morning and see what happens. Start taking a pill now and come back after an hour.

I blindly followed this fellow, if he asked me to take my shirt off and walk around Manhattan I would do it.

So down I went after taking that pill, from 7th Avenue New York I kept walking towards Times Square, just looking at my watch and to see how much time I needed to spend outside, I still remember the chilly wintery days and they used to make my happy, so I kept walking enjoying the new York scenery and then when the time was up, I came back up to his office and I said, I feel a lot of energy coming up to my brain, and he told me take it each morning and see if your results are going to change as you are now desperate to get back.

In the week that followed again I was sitting in his office and I had again got a warning from him that enough is enough and he is going to close my account and give me a check, he told me you are not ready to trade, he said that the way you are making money it is not done, and he wrote me a check for nearly a million which I deposited in the chase bank branch near my office that same evening.

The banking clerk jumped from her seat when she saw that amount of check but I was calm.

The real essence is that this drug can help you a tonne, it can help in bringing about a positive change in you, start with taking 10mg when you wake up, not more than 10mg because it can cause some side effects too, some people take 20mg it depends on what your body type is and what gives you the max boost.

You will notice that you will get a lot done, the road blocks are clearing away, your mind is getting clearer, it may be possible that you are not able to get this drug or get a prescription for it, and it is lame how the government plays the big daddy and controls everything.

If you cannot get it or any generic drug Modafinil then simply email me and I will help you get it delivered to your address without a prescription.

Simply email me with subject Modafinil and ask me cost and payment instructions.

Email   me   at
FreemanFromZero@gmail.com

5 DROPSHIPPING YOUR WAY TO RISE FROM ZERO

Just imagine for a moment how big is the consumer market.

People around the world are looking for things to buy, things to get for their families which is going to give them mental satisfaction, which is going to make them or their families happy.

It is a very big market, now if you can grab even the tiniest bit of that market it is going to be huge.

In a simple sense let me give you an

example of Drop Shipping.

So I identified a performance improving drug which was in high demand in my country and people from all walks of competitive arenas were vying for that, and in my country it was selling for over a thousand dollars, and when I researched the prices in another developing country I was shocked to know that it was available for just 10 dollars.

So I made a few contacts in that country and set up a channel which would deliver this to me, when I placed an order with them.

It is not exactly like drop shipping in which the seller directly sends the goods to your purchaser, but in this scenario I was delivering in my home country myself.

Let me explain I created a YouTube channel, a blog detailing the various benefits that could be obtained by this miracle drug and all the resources that I used in social media were freely available and I did not need to spend even a single dollar. People were interested in the product and were calling me, and I told them that I will deliver to them and they need to pay me this much.

It needs to be a personal relationship between you and the purchaser, also you need to create your own branding for that product so that your purchaser doesn't feel cheated.

So I was procuring for 100 dollars from overseas what was being sold in the local market for 1000 dollars and I was selling it for 300 dollars.

People needed it badly and when they figured it was well within their reach and only thing is delivery time they were accepting and happy to get it.

So I would get paid 300 dollars, and I would ship the product to them, the first order took 2 weeks, but from the profits I made on the first order, I was able to order in advance this item, and I was able to deliver them in time, I also figured it out that by using Adsense my sales skyrocketed.

I found out that for 50 every 50 dollars spent I would get at least 1 sale. So now my inputs were 150 dollars and I was netting a 150 dollars net profit.

In a month I was sitting on a pile of cash that people would make in six months which is a very nice thing.

This gives you a very good example on how to create businesses by just investing your time and energy and not spending any money upfront and testing to see if it is going to work or not.

I will always follow Warren Buffet's first rule never lose money. And to never forget rule number 1. If something is made to fly it will, if something is not made to fly even if you put a billion dollars after it, it won't.

I don't want to be that person who loses in business ventures, that's the reason and the same strategy I want you to learn. I can get a jazzy website, I can get superior developers to build my website, I can get ten guys who will write this book or make me a great cover, but that will defeat the purpose of this project.

This entire project from blog to social media content, to book and cover design is made using free tools. I have not put even a single dollar but with this project I want you to have an impact on your mind, I want you to quit your job and start generating value for yourself by building business ventures in the things that you are knowledgeable. I want to set you free.

If you have any doubts or you want a one one one live stream with me then email me at freemanfromzero@gmail.com and let me help you become a freeman from zero.

I will figure out what your passions are and what your core strengths are and let me figure out a system for you that helps you get value and money for your time, energy, creativity and business acumen.

Justs by reading books you cannot succeed, also if you think that you need a super star like Google founder or Facebook founder who is going to spoon feed you then that's not going to happen as these people have already so much going on, so you need to find a mentor you trust and get started.

If you want to know in details on how you can get started with drop shipping and some real know how then contact me for my personal course.

6 ONCE YOU HAVE MADE 1000 DOLLARS, ANOTHER PASSIVE STREAM

Passive stream of income is something that you get by investing very little time and energy.

So I have given you several options to raise your first thousand dollars, there are a thousand topics on which you can create your self published course, you can create a youtube channel, or you can create a drop shipping business, or if you can't do the above then you can take simple jobs like tuitions, or simple store jobs and within a short period of time you will have a thousand dollars if you save.

Remember you never need to take any risk with your money because let me get this point straight in you that money is the hardest thing to get if you lose it. Earning money is very hard, making money is very easy, the world is running on money and it is going to be very easy to lose money in this world.

I am never going to tell you to take risks, even for my business ventures I won't put down any money. I may have a million dollars sitting in assets but I won't put even a 100 dollars because the truth of the matter is if there is value in a venture, it will be realized if you put time and energy, most places where you need to put money to make a lot are fake, and you can lose all the money.

Also what is the problem from starting from 0, and to reinvest what you get, this way your personal finances are not impacted, and you are not in a situation where you need to use the money that you are earning.

So in essence if you get 500 dollars you can reinvest the entire amount, this also helps to validate if it is a revenue generating business.

If my business can earn 100k dollars I would have no problem investing 100k dollars back in the same business, and this way you need to think about business, you don't need to put money upfront.

So now let's get back to this chapter, say you have a 1000 dollars lying extra, and you have made revenue streams that are earning for you, now why to keep money lying useless.

What you can do is use classifieds and put ads for free that you have this latest games consoles available for rent and see the response, if people contact you that they need it, build a list of the people enquiring, once you have built a list of 100 people, then go and buy consoles from the extra money lying with you, and connect back with the same 100 people who were looking to rent most probably these same people would not have bought the console and would rent your console as per their schedule sooner or later.

In their initial query just mention that you don't have the consoles and are already rented and you will contact them when consoles will be available for rent. This way before buying any rental equipment you will have a clear idea as to what is going to be the response for your rental business. And if the response is cold go the next idea and see where people need help and do that.

Also validation will help you save a lot of money, frustration and lost time by investing very little time and energy and putting no money upfront.

7 TURNING TEN THOUSAND DOLLARS TO A MILLION IDEA

So by this time and before you read this chapter you have built income streams, you have passive income flowing in, you find that after your expenses and backup fund you have extra ten thousand dollars lying in your account.

I am never a proponent of letting money sit idle, it feels so wasteful of letting money sit idle which would have been used in generating more value.

Plus I have never invested or taken risks with money in a new venture, the new venture must start from the grass root level and with profits it needs to build up.

Market research is extremely important, you want to find out before-hand if what you are investing into is going to be successful or not.

There are big firms dedicated to finding out if what your next product is going to be a success or not, what is going to be the market response for it, how much sales you can expect, one example of such a company is Nielsen.

So now you are hearing from me how to turn ten grand to a million, that's like a one in a hundred chance if everything was even. But in real world value is lost very quickly, and mostly it becomes a one in a thousand chance, because every person, every organization, the government needs money to run. Value keeps getting lost, there are taxes that need to be paid, there are indirect taxes that need to be paid. Government is a big value sucking machine, and no wonder Government jobs are so much sought after.

So let's get back how to turn ten k to a million. The answer is simple: harness the power of internet. Scale up quickly when you find that there is a value.

You need to form a company, a separate entity focusing on this business.

You need to build a brand and it is going to take the help of several entities and people who will register your company, do branding for you, create your own unique logo, get you phone number, then you need an office which will build trust in the minds of your purchasers.

Trust me from the smallest level you can achieve this all in ten k dollars.

Getting your own office, getting your own brand, getting your own company registered is going to build trust in the minds of consumers, consumers are extremely smart, they have been burnt enough times to know whom to trust and who not to trust.

You cannot befol the consumers and if you still do manage to do there is going to be a legal framework which is going to come after you. Consumers know this and hence the trust builds.

If you can generate value for these people and keep reinvesting the value that you get back in the same business before you know it, it is going to be a million dollar business.

Cash flow is the most important thing, you need to manage cash flow, and make sure there is always plenty because that is the single point which can choke your business and make you gather debt which will have high interest.

Cash flow troubles have turned billionaires to millionaires take example of Vijay Mallaya or Anil Ambani who kept on taking debts and when the market slumped and the value of their businesses eroded were sitting under mountains of debt.

In a span of a 5 or 6 years Anil Ambani turned to dust 45 billion dollars and how he managed to achieve that I cannot explain.

Take the case of Kanye West or so many others who overestimated themselves kept on taking debts and when business or economy slumped or the value of their business eroded, looked like moles to the mountain of debts they took.

The rule is simple: if something is meant to fly it will and if something is not meant to fly and even if you put a billion dollars behind it it won't.

So now let's come back to the topic of turning ten thousand dollars into a million. You have formed your own company, you have built a brand, you now identify markets where the things are very cheap, manufacturing costs are very low, China! you figured it out!

There are so many companies in the USA that are selling locally and importing things from China.

You can import toys, robots, drones, cosmetic care products, rebrand them and sell.

Of course you need to do proper research and validation.

If you can sell to ten thousand consumers and from the sales you can make a net profit of 100 dollars each then you can make a million easily.

8 Investing Large Amounts And Difference Between Investing And Gambling

So you have a large amount, a large amount is defined as something that would take years of a normal job to acquire.

If this fails it means years of effort is going to waste.

You never want this to happen and such amounts are best kept secured in assets like real estate.

You cannot invest in large amounts which is a major part of your net worth in stocks and think it secure, because what the price of a company is going to be tomorrow, you never know.

But you do know that tomorrow the real estate price of the house you bought is not going to be anything much different.

Real estate has always been one of the safest investments and it also has made the most millionaires around the world.

Over a period of time in developing areas the real estate rates have always beat inflation and have provided a lot of value to the investors.

Hence if you are seeking to invest large amounts chose to invest in real estate.

Investing in under developed and developing areas and leaving the investment for a long time is a sure shot way to create a multi bagger investment.

And even if you do not multiply your money in a real estate investment, you know that real estate cannot be stolen like crypto, it cannot lose 30 percent value overnight like crypto.

Plus if you have passive income streams and you can pay down a large part of downpayment of the house, you can easily get loans by showing your income proof, and that you have a stable income and that the house investment will be paid for.

Gambling is the number 1 wealth destroyer anytime you are taking risk, you are opening the doors to a disaster, you escape one time, you escape 20 times but on the 21st time a disaster happens.

Even if you took a percent chance for a disaster then it can happen and leave you in deep trouble, and I don't understand people that keep on buying lottery tickets for a major part of their disposable incomes for a 99.999999% chance of failure. It's stupid would you agree?

These are the same people who have been misguided about money and finances, they are lazy and they do not want to work, they want to take a chance and hope and pray that they get rich.

Take for example Donald Trump the current president of America he and his father always worked in real estate and that's how they made billions. When real estate came crashing down, Trump ran into the gaming business and would later recover it all with having his banking partners defer his loans and having them loan an additional 65 million dollars.

9 USING ESSENTIAL TOOLS AVAILABLE FOR FREE IN BUILDING YOUR BUSINESS

The most important thing in today's businesses are social media tools. Facebook, LinkedIn, Blogs, WhatsApp, Instagram, YouTube has made it very easy for people to connect and get connected to you.

All you need is the will to connect to others and you will get connected to the people, you can connect your business to the people.

So for this startup business let me tell you

again I have not put even a single dollar, I have opted for a free Wix blog website, I have opted for free self publishing using Amazon Kindle, I have also used it's free cover creator.

The image for cover has come from Pixabay which is a completely free image sharing service.

Plus the usual social media tools like Facebook, LinkedIn, Twitter, Instagram, Email will build your brand and will give maximum amount of people to connect with you.

Then there are google groups which you can use to connect even more people.

With LinkedIn it is very easy to connect to the other greats in your industry and build trust among your followers.

LinkedIn may also help you connect with potential investors in your business. You can send messages to people whom it would be impossible to meet in real life.

You can get connected with these people and build a strong network. What happens is that few industry leaders have a lot of followers and if they take a liking to your product or offering and they post a message about it, suddenly you will see a spurt in your sales.

Plus before you start anything you need to validate, if this idea or project is worth to invest your time and energy.

The results will be very clear very soon, think about 10 business or book ideas and create surveys for people or create blog posts regarding those ten topics and the topic on which you find the max hits, you can be sure that people are interested in it.

Also you can take the help of Google Trends going after the hottest topics or those topics which are quickly emerging and having tremendous growth are good areas to invest time and energy.

Better to be safer first then sorry

A lot of times what happens is people will jump head first in business, and invest a lot of money, energy and time.

After the entire project will be done they will then start thinking why I am not getting any response for it.

Then the entire project kind of gets shelved, abandoned or ignored, and whatever resources have been put in it become wasted.

To prevent this kind of scenario people need to do research.

Do note that all big companies who will be spending very large amounts on their consumer products also do not just jump blindly, they will pay firms which will analyze in advance the success or fail ratios of their products, what is going to be the estimated demand, what is the competition like, how much market share they can grab.

Very similar analysis is needed for individuals starting their own businesses, or ventures or even eBooks, even if you are thinking of starting a blog, find out what people are passionate about, which blogs are earning huge and which kind of blogs are neglected.

With this approach you will be much more successful.

10 LET'S GET STARTED

It's time! The reason you bought this book is because you have something unfulfilled in your life.

You are unhappy from your job, you feel trapped by capitalism, you have great ideas and you haven't been able to work on them.

It's the best time to join Freeman and become a freeman yourself.

When you connect with me you connect to a growing society of people who are like minded and who are looking to start their own ventures, projects, startups.

Several people that I know have raised millions in venture funding.

Several have sold their companies and are now sitting on mountains of cash looking to invest.

When you join me, you are connecting with a mentor who is going to answer any questions that you have, who can guide you building your startup on a personal level.

You can live stream, Skype, connect with me personally by email, phone, you can ask me if this business idea is good or not.

So basically you can consult with me, and I can be your business consultant, and remember with tonnes of experience in serial entrepreneurs, you can never go wrong in consulting from me.

The advice that you get is going to be precious.

Email me exactly what you are looking for, what you are looking forward to build, and for just 150 dollars we can connect with each other and you can get quality guidance and support. Per hour right now I am charging 50 dollars.

So in this course you have any doubts, or need more information feel free to connect with me, email me at FreemanFromZero@gmail.com

ABOUT THE AUTHOR

Hello, I can be contacted on
FreemanFromZero@gmail.com Get
connected to our community, learn and
share!

Get inspired by dozens of inspiring stories
of my readers and wannabe
entrepreneurs. Email me and you will be
joined on the mailing list.

PLus finally if this book helped you give it
a positive review right now!